WHO'S IN THE DRIVER'S SEAT?

Using Spirit to Lead Successfully

SANDY GLUCKMAN, Ph.D.

WHO'S
IN THE
DRIVER'S
SEAT?

Using Spirit to Lead Successfully

Inquiries regarding permission for use of the material contained in this book should be addressed to:

CornerStone Leadership Institute
P.O. Box 764087
Dallas, TX 75376
888.789.LEAD

Printed in the United States of America
ISBN: 0-9788137-6-6

Credits

Design, art direction, and production — Melissa Monogue, Back Porch Creative, Plano, TX
info@BackPorchCreative.com

Copy Editor — Kathleen Green, Positively Proofed, Plano, TX
info@PositivelyProofed.com

Table of Contents

SECTION 1

INTRODUCTION

Switching Them On

Using Spirit as the Key

A prominent leader was once asked how many people worked on his team.

"About half of them," he promptly replied.

Was he just being funny or had he read the latest research?

According to the Gallup organization, less than half of today's employees act in ways that create positive customer experiences and business success for their organizations! That leaves about 22 million switched-off employees, costing the American economy as much as $350 billion a year. This challenging reality is causing leaders at all levels to ask themselves:

How do we build switched-on teams?

How can we connect with our teams so they energetically embrace the organization's goals as their own?

How can we spark a passion for accountability and superior performance in every member of the team?

Who's in the Driver's Seat provides a roadmap to switching on employees to achieve superior performance ... and superior, sustainable results. When employees feel switched on, they enhance their organization's success in numerous and measurable ways. They "get" the vision and make a commitment to quality and growth. They feel good about the future, love the work they do, produce more, are better communicators, enjoy challenges and switch customers on.

Switched-on employees are accountable for their role in making customers happy and become valuable assets to your organization.

Since 70 percent of all buying decisions are based on a positive human interaction, switched-on employees play a critical role in building and sustaining a loyal customer base.

Switched-off employees, on the other hand, create switched-off customers. Employees who feel emotionally switched-off cannot be accountable. Their determination to succeed and desire to engage is also switched off. They feel tired and lethargic. The little energy they do have goes into finding ways to cope. Their vision is survival. They don't optimize their intelligence and talents. Instead, they just go through the motions, feeling disconnected from their colleagues and the organization's goals.

Spirit is the key

So what gives switched-on teams the edge? What makes them capable of superior performance? What do they have that switched-off employees don't have?

They have spirit. When they work with spirit, they take their performance to the next level.

Let's use a familiar analogy: Think of the great spirit found in a winning sports team. The players are focused, forceful, determined, courageous, skilled, gutsy, confident, and yet, humble. They envision themselves as winners, have supreme belief in their own talent and the talent of the other team members and are driven to achieve a shared dream. They cheer each other on every step of the way. These players are totally switched on and play as one. **Their spirited selves are in the driver's seat.**

When we work or play with spirit in the driver's seat, we are filled with positive emotions. We are optimistic and enthusiastic. We feel switched on and energized!

It's different with losing teams. Unable to pull together, these team members play with ego, not with spirit. The members of losing teams are self-serving, pulling in different directions. Each is focused on his or her own personal agenda. Their egos create petty distractions and negative emotions, which get in the way of winning. They are switched off from their powerful, spirited selves. **Losing teams have their egos in the driver's seat.** No matter how gifted these players may be, they don't have the "mojo" that comes from spirit.

Switched-on teams are spirited teams, and spirited teams have special abilities that produce extraordinary performance resulting in spirited customers. Spirited customers become fans of your organization and spend more money with you. They also love to tell others about your products and services.

Just as a spirited team wins games and fans, so a spirited work force creates loyal customers and boosts sales.

More than ever before, leaders know that the ratio between switched-on and switched-off employees is a key indicator of company performance. Knowing how to switch others on is no longer an option. It's a critical leadership competence and ability that will set your organization apart from your competition.

So how do leaders switch their teams on?

Surprisingly, it's a simple and common skill, but one of the most underused in the leadership toolbox. Connect with employees and others in a way that creates positive emotions. In fact, a study by Gallup found the most productive workgroups had at least a 3-to-1 ratio of positive to negative interactions. Anything less than 3-to-1, and the group's productivity decreased significantly. So, what does that tell us? A team with 3-to-1 positive to negative interactions, or better yet, a 5-to-1 or 10-to-1 ratio is clearly switched on.

Why is positive emotion the key to switching others on?

If we deconstruct the word, 'e-motion,' we find that emotions create movement, emotions make things happen. Here's how it works: Positive feelings convert into positive energy. Positive energy is spirit. Spirited employees think and act in in-spirit-ed (inspired) ways. To use the words of the famous football coach, Vince Lombardi, spirited teams have "the will to win and the will to excel."

So why do so many leaders lack this spirit and switch off their employees? The answer is *ego*.

Ego is the enemy of spirit. When ego is in the driver's seat, spirit becomes a passenger. Ego-driven leaders create negative feelings, which switch off others. When we are switched off, we are dis-spirited. Dis-spirited people are incapable of delivering positive results.

There are millions of employees who have been switched off by leaders who drive with their egos in the driver's seat. Most of these employees have great potential, but without spirit, they cannot convert their potential into positive performance. No matter how educated and experienced we are, as leaders, if our ego is in the driver's seat, we are switching others off and we have given up the right to expect superior results from those we lead.

In every single interaction we have a choice:

We can choose to respond with

The Spirited Self

OR

Just as every coin has two sides and only one side can be up at any one time, each of us has two sides. One side of our being is the *spirited self* – courageous, potent and real. The other side is the *ego self* – a non-authentic, self-protective public image. **Only one of these two sides can be in the driver's seat at any one time.**

When our spirited self is in the driver's seat, we connect with others and create positive emotions – like optimism, exhilaration, enthusiasm and determination. However, when our ego is in the driver's seat, we will do and say things that cause others to feel cynical, skeptical and discouraged. The ego makes employees feel angry, sad or afraid. To cope with these negative emotions that the ego-driven leader triggers in them, employees shut down and then switch off.

Most people are familiar with IQ and EQ. IQ is how the logical mind thinks. EQ is how the emotional mind thinks. Exciting new research recently discovered the brain possesses a third intelligence called SQ. SQ is how the spirited mind thinks and is the basis of in-spirit-ed (inspired) thinking.

The moment we become aware the ego is driving us and we consciously shift our ego into the passenger seat, we automatically activate spirit. Now, our in-spirit-ed intelligence – SQ – is engaged and we find ourselves capable of producing extraordinary results.

Ego sees the world as limited, narrow, polarized and threatening. SQ converts our limited, ego interpretation of events and information into a 360-degree view, revealing possibilities that ego with IQ and EQ cannot compute. SQ is free of black-and-white, either/or, right-or-wrong thinking. These are boundaries imposed by ego.

With spirit in the driver's seat, we think beyond these boundaries. Now we have the mental and emotional stamina to put our challenges into a broader perspective and see what new opportunities this brings to light. Then we have the courage to change the rules, transform the situation and create an environment that encourages and supports progress.

This remarkable intelligence is available to everyone, regardless of education or experience. But we can only access our SQ when our spirited self is in the driver's seat and our ego is in the passenger seat.

Spirited leaders make the most of all three intelligences. They gather the facts and figures with IQ, apply their EQ to manage the emotional issues and use SQ to inspire spirit in others. SQ also facilitates inspired strategic and tactical decisions, brings about inspired conversations and drives inspired action and accountability.

The Cost of Ego

The cost of ego shows up every moment of every day in every office, every meeting room, around every boardroom table, at the water cooler – any place where people gather. Ego costs can be measured in wasted time, underutilized talent, loss of information, poor decisions, lost opportunities and in the cost of medications for physical and emotional distress.

A 20-year study of more than 400 decisions made by top managers revealed 50 percent of all business decisions failed.

One-third of these failed because of ego. In his book, *Good to Great*, Jim Collins writes: "In over two-thirds of comparison cases (average/good companies), we noted the presence of gargantuan personal ego that contributed to the demise or continued mediocrity of the company."

In this book, we'll explore what happens to organizations and teams when leaders have their ego or their spirit in the driver's seat. We'll also show how ego and spirit have the power to switch employees on or off. Every leader is responsible for understanding how spirit and ego impacts others and, in turn, directly impacts their organization's performance.

Who's in the Driver's Seat offers practical actions to create and hone Spirited Leadership. With spirit in the driver's seat and ego in the passenger seat, spirited leaders can create a switched-on work force, one that enthusiastically takes responsibility for delivering remarkable performance.

Get ready to discover "Who's in Your Driver's Seat!"

1

Introducing Our Drivers

Recognizing Your SELF in George and Dave

George and Dave are managers in the same company, working in different departments. Both are in their late 30s, and are respected for their technical and academic expertise in their respective fields. Both joined the company seven years ago and have risen in the ranks. The difference? George's team members describe him as a red convertible while Dave's team sees him as being more like a hybrid. Let me tell you why.

On one particular Friday, George is sitting in the cafeteria having lunch with Tom, a colleague from another department. George is telling Tom he's having a tough time getting the employees in his department to take accountability for their roles in the company's new strategy. "They don't seem to want to apply themselves and are not producing the measures of success they agreed to deliver," he says, "and I'm frustrated. Very few participate in meetings," George continues to complain. "It's as though they're half dead – and it makes me crazy. I find myself banging on the table, challenging them to come up with something intelligent to say, but they just don't get it!"

What George isn't telling Tom is this is actually not a new problem. He's had this problem since he became a manager several years ago.

George has been able to keep his job, up to now, because he has superb marketing skills. However, his superiors have advised him to get a personal coach, hoping this will help him address these managerial challenges. But George has resisted this, mainly because he doesn't believe he needs coaching. He believes the problem lies with "them." "If it weren't so costly on so many levels," he tells Tom, "I would solve the problem by hiring a bunch of new people."

GEORGE - THE RED CONVERTIBLE

Tom's brother-in-law, Ted, works in George's department. Listening to George at the lunch table, Tom can't help thinking about the numerous times Ted had asked him for advice about how to cope with what he refers to as George's "ego."

Unfortunately, George is perceived by his department as being self-righteous, always acting as though he has all the answers and throwing temper tantrums, calling them "half dead" and telling them they will never succeed. This switches them off.

His team compares George to the red, two-seater sports car he drives – flashy, aggressive, "in your face," with just enough space for George and his briefcase.

Ted had also told Tom he and his co-workers have tried, tactfully, to tell George his behavior is switching them off and affecting their ability to be productive. But George isn't getting the message. In fact, he's such a bad listener, he's never heard what they are telling him. He's never noticed his team is becoming angrier and more frustrated. Nor does he realize his team's way of coping is to become turned off and tuned out. As a result, they're doing just enough to get by. They are going through the motions and are totally disengaged from George, from each other and from the organization's goals.

The one place they can safely express their true views is in the employee survey because it's completely anonymous. Not surprisingly, George consistently scores poorly on the employee surveys. This concerns him because a part of his incentive package depends on the survey's results. The lower George scores on the employee surveys, the more George's boss confronts him about the problems in his department. And the angrier George gets with his team about their lack of accountability, the more switched off and shut down they become.

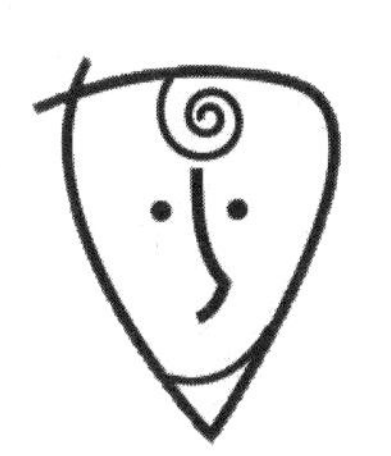

DAVE – THE HYBRID CAR

Then there's Dave.

Down the hall on the south side of the building is Dave's office. He's passionate about asking his team for feedback. Two weeks ago, he asked them an unusual question: "If you used a car to describe me, which one would you choose and why?"

His team members all agreed the hybrid best symbolized Dave because of his focus on the larger purpose, his emphasis on efficiency and his dream of making the department an even better place to work.

What's most striking about Dave is his strong self-confidence, mixed with an equally strong dose of humility. His open, interactive and collaborative style inspires the respect and commitment of everyone he works with. He also has the knack of being able to tell others exactly what he expects in a way that makes them want to rush off and do it in the quickest and smartest way they can. He knows just how to switch on his team.

If you popped into Dave's department, you would immediately be aware of an enthusiastic spirit and a contagious energy. Ask his team members about the strategy, and they'll tell you, with great clarity, about the organization's vision and goals and how their function supports this.

If you ask them about Dave, they'll talk about how much they enjoy the way Dave keeps pushing the envelope because they know that he will support them every inch of the way in achieving challenging goals.

On this particular day, while George is complaining to Tom over lunch, Dave is having a working lunch with his team. While they munch on the delicious sandwiches Dave has ordered from the deli, he thanks them for their excellent scores on the employee survey and then addresses two areas where he received lower ratings than he expected. Now he wants to know exactly what he's doing that isn't working and what he can do to improve this.

At about the same time George and Dave are eating lunch with their teams, Dave's boss, Matt, and George's boss, Fred, are in meetings as well. They are in different parts of the building meeting with the vice presidents to whom they report.

Dave's boss is having a great meeting. The vice president congratulates him on achieving his quarterly goals. Matt knows he looks good because Dave's department is producing exceptional results. And Matt loves his incentive bonus!

George's boss isn't faring as well – mainly because he's trying to explain to his VP why, as George's leader, he is unable to obtain better performance from George and his team.

How often have we seen this happen: two equally educated people in the same company with the same CEO, the same corporate vision, values and strategic goals, working within the same corporate culture, with the same access to resources and yet, one department is thriving while another one isn't?

So What's the Difference Between Dave and George?

If you ask others who know George and Dave, they'll tell you the difference between them can be described by one word: *Ego*. With George's ego in the driver's seat, it switches others off and sabotages his ability to connect with his team. Dave, on the other hand, has his spirit in the driver's seat and ego in the passenger seat, which means he has a spirited, winning team.

Here's a summary of the distinguishing qualities of Dave and George's teams. Notice what happens to the team when George's ego is in the driver's seat. Compare this to what happens when Dave's ego is in the passenger seat.

George's Team is Switched Off

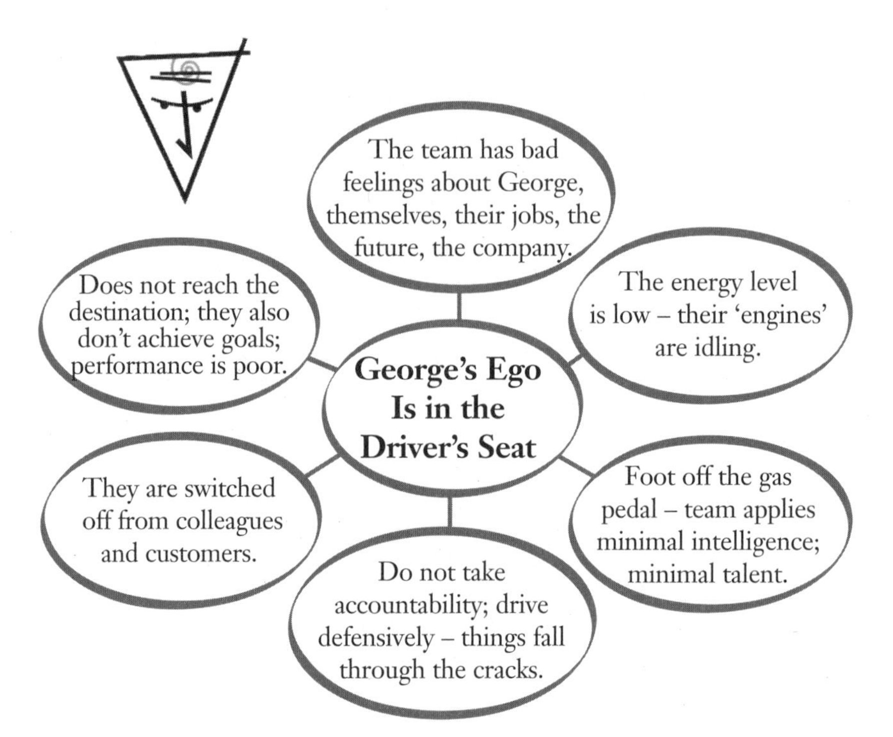

Dave's Team is Switched On

Spirit Is a Core Leadership Competence

Although decision makers with their ego in the driver's seat usually create the perception that they are confident and in control, many of these same leaders are actually insecure. They are frightened about what others will think about them, and their egos cause them to act like bullies and make poor decisions.

It's important to look at the huge impact leaders and their egos have on the growth or decline of organizations, people, families, communities ... even countries. It's also important to be aware of the critical role played by spirit and to have the courage to include spirit as a core leadership competence and business imperative.

When role models at senior leadership levels have spirit in the driver's seat, this encourages an ever-expanding cycle of spirited behavior throughout the organization. Spirited leadership quashes power games, boardroom games, strategy games and money games that ego and lack of SQ nurture. Making spirit a core leadership competence will also call a halt to the non-productive, energy-sapping, uncreative, dignity-destroying behaviors many teams – at all levels – contend with from their leaders.

Think of all the meetings you've attended where people were afraid to challenge the status quo, where there was low participation, low ownership and accountability, little enthusiasm, no creative energy, mediocre decision making and execution and much passing the buck.

Now, total the hours of these meetings per month and how many people attend these meetings. Then, take an average of the salaries involved and calculate the cost of the lack of spirit. Multiply that by the number of ego-driven managers in the company and the cost is, no doubt, staggering.

It's a fact! Leaders riding with their ego in the driver's seat can make or break companies and the spirit of the people in them. Don't deny, condone or avoid this reality any longer. Instead of spending millions of dollars on programs, attempting to fix the dysfunctions these ego-driven leaders create, why not go back to basics and remedy the problem where it starts – by teaching leaders at all levels how to put spirit in the driver's seat and ego in the passenger seat.

SECTION 2

Putting Spirit in the Driver's Seat

2

The Owner's Manual

Choosing Who's in the Driver's Seat

Ever wonder why some leaders have no need for ego while others function most of the time with ego in the driver's seat? Or, why leaders keep leading with ego when doing this gets them the opposite result they are striving for? And, why is it so hard to get through to a leader whose ego is driving?

Here are the answers to these important questions.

WE ARE BORN WITH SPIRIT.
WE CANNOT BE BORN WITH EGO.

At birth – and for a short time afterward – we do not have an ego self at all. We are simply highly spirited little children who are naturally genuine, spontaneous, curious, confident and vulnerable. Then, in order to fit in, we develop a social personality we sometimes use when we need to behave in ways we think will be more acceptable to others.

That's how the ego personality comes into being. On the one hand, this means that, as kids, the ego self helps us get lots of approval. On the other hand, every time we use the ego, we are being disloyal to our spirited self.

It also means we learned to be non-authentic because the ego is the non-authentic part of us. Over the years, we carry this social personality around with us and put the authentic spirited self in the passenger seat, just so others will approve of us.

Then, one day we join an organization and become the leader of a team. Now we have a choice. Do we lead the team with ego in the driver's seat or do we put spirit behind the wheel?

The challenge? There are so many people watching us and judging us. When we are concerned about looking good in the eyes of others, there's a chance that, just as we did as children, we will use the ego personality as leaders. This is because – **unlike the spirited self that is motivated from the inside-out – the ego is motivated from the outside-in**.

THE CHOICE IS YOURS

Remember the coin? If you throw a coin up in the air, it sometimes lands heads up and, other times, tails up. It's the same way with us. On some occasions we're "ego side up" and the ego self is in the driver's seat. On other occasions, we are "spirit side up" and the real self is in the driver's seat.

Whether spirit or ego is driving depends on how safe – or unsafe – we feel in the situation or relationship. There are some situations where we feel safe enough to be our authentic, spirited self without any pretense. In these situations, the ego self is a passenger. There are, however, those situations in which we feel threatened and the ego is in the driver's seat, doing and saying whatever is necessary to protect us.

There is one essential difference between a two-sided coin and our two-sided beings: We get to choose "which side is up!"

Although the driver and the passenger can change in different situations, here's the reality: we each have a dominant driver that takes control in most situations. If our dominant driver is ego, it's important that we recognize this and deliberately and consciously choose to put the spirited self in the driver's seat on all occasions.

Making this choice is not easy, however, because we have used the ego self so often. By the time we become adults, we find it difficult to differentiate between the real self and the public self. We believe our ego is who we really are, but this is not true. So the first step is to discover the difference between our ego self and our spirited self.

EGO CREATES BLIND SPOTS

The journey to discover who is in the driver's seat starts with awareness.

The challenge is that ego has a low level of awareness. Having awareness is a function of being spirited. In fact, the more dominant our ego is, the lower our level of awareness is. For leaders who lead with ego, this means they usually wear blinders, have closed minds and don't want to hear anything that will cause them discomfort.

Ego-driven leaders are also the very people who are in denial about having ego and that their ego is switching others off.

I was on a plane recently and experienced an example of someone who, obviously, had never been given any feedback about himself. I was shown to my seat by the flight attendant and, as I sat down, the man sitting next to me turned to his son and said, "Oh darn!"

I asked him if there was a problem, and he said, "I was hoping the seat would remain empty." So I promised him if the plane wasn't full, I would move.

A few minutes later, a woman boarded the plane carrying a baby and sat down a few seats away from us. "Oh no!" the man next to me said out loud. "That baby is going to squawk all the way and ruin our trip." He then picked up the magazine provided by the airline and, after quickly paging through it, announced, "These things are always full of rubbish. Who cares who Mel Gibson was last seen chatting with?"

The flight attendant then began instructions on what to do in case of an emergency, and the man turned to his son and said, "Look at that woman. If an accident did happen, she would probably be the first to panic."

That's when I thought to myself, "Good grief! Didn't anybody care enough about this guy to tell him about how he was coming across?"

We took off and, since there were no empty seats, he must have decided to make the best of it, so he turned to me and said, "What do you do with your life?"

"I am a consultant," I responded.

He thought for a moment and then said, "You really must meet some funny types!"

So here's the dilemma this story poses: If you are one of those people hiding the truth about your ego – from yourself – the people around you would find it difficult to give you feedback – you would be blind to the fact that your ego is in the driver's seat. You would probably think you're okay and others are the problem. You'd also believe you are honest with yourself and others – that your style is encouraging and motivating, and the team is lucky to have you! How would you ever know this is, really, your ego hiding the truth from you?

Even as you read this – and I write this – our egos could be playing tricks with both of us. What if we don't know that we don't know? And what if we don't want to hear what we don't want to hear? We would be stuck with our ego in the driver's seat and our teams would be switched off and unproductive.

SAY 'HI' TO YOUR EGO

There is only one way to eliminate blind spots – and that's through courageous awareness.

Spirited leaders face the facts, head on, and admit they have an ego. So, begin with the intellectual awareness that ego is not something to be embarrassed about. We all have ego and when we feel uncomfortable, we use our ego to protect our self-esteem. This is an inescapable fact. With this awareness, the first step is to say "hi" to your ego.

The next step is to gain awareness of how your ego looks and sounds. What does it do and say when it is in the driver's seat? Now, here you'll collide with an awareness deadlock created by the ego. To get around this, let others be your mirror, your eyes and your ears.

If you were driving a car with a blind spot, you would be sure to look around, periodically scanning the space around you. As a leader, be courageous and ask others for feedback – from those who report to you, your colleagues, your manager and your golf buddies. Compare your self-perception with the perception of others.

There are, however, two prerequisites for this exercise. First, it's vital you only ask those who have courage and are not afraid to be honest. Secondly, you must express the request for feedback using spirited language. Here's an example: "Joe, I am on a personal improvement drive and would appreciate some really open, honest feedback. What are some of the things you think I could do differently that would have a more positive impact on you and others? I'm interested in knowing what I may be doing that switches you and others off. Then, tell me what I could be doing to create a more switched-on team."

Would this send a powerful message to Joe?

Once you're aware of your ego behaviors – those seen and felt by others – you're now in a position to manage your ego, using the tools offered in the chapters that follow.

Here's the deal about the ego. It is never going away! And, it's okay to have the ego in the driver's seat on some occasions. However, there are three important questions you should ask yourself – and answer:

1. Which of the two sides of you is in the driver's seat most of the time?

2. Do you know how to recognize whether the ego self or spirited self is driving?

3. Are you in charge – do you choose the driver?

The following chapters offer you behavioral and language clues to help you recognize some of what your ego says and does when it's in the driver's seat.

3

Taking Control of the Wheel

Watch Your Behavior

Bill is a brilliant, financially struggling student. He has wild hair, wears a T-shirt with holes in it, jeans and old shoes with no socks. This has been his wardrobe for his entire four years of college.

One Sunday, feeling the need for support, Bill decides to visit the conservative church across the street from campus. He has wanted to do this for a long while but – being dressed the way he always was – was afraid of offending the well-dressed parishioners.

The service has already started and so Bill starts down the aisle, looking for a seat, but the church is completely packed and there is not a single seat available. By now, everyone is looking very uncomfortable and there is the sound of whispering as people share remarks with each other.

Bill gets closer and closer to the pulpit and when he realizes that he cannot find a seat, he squats down and sits on the carpet. (Although perfectly acceptable behavior at a college fellowship, trust me, this had never happened in this church before.)

By now the tension in the air is thick. About this time, the minister realizes a deacon is slowly making his way toward Bill from the back of the church. The deacon is in his 80s, a godly man, very elegant, very dignified, and very courtly. He walks with a cane and, as he starts walking to this boy, everyone is thinking to themselves, "I can't blame him for what he is about to do."

It takes a long time for the deacon to reach the boy. The church is utterly silent except for the clicking of the man's cane. All eyes are focused on him. The minister stops preaching, mid-sermon, waiting for the deacon to do what he is going to do.

As he reaches the boy, this elderly man drops his cane on the floor and, with great difficulty, lowers himself and sits down next to Bill, worshiping with him so he won't be alone. Everyone chokes with emotion.

When the minister gains control, he says, "What I'm about to preach, you will never remember. What you have just seen, you will never forget. Be careful how you behave. You may be the only Bible some people will ever read."

Leading at the Intersection

Clearly, the deacon's spirited self was in the driver's seat. He could have responded with ego, as the congregants thought he might, and the story would be very different.

Just as members of the team would watch and listen very carefully at an intersection before making a move, so they are watching you, their leader. You are their traffic light, giving them a red light or a green light. They are watching what you do, listening to what you say and then filtering this information through their emotions.

Basically they will come to one vital conclusion: What my boss does and says makes me feel good and switches me on. Or, they will conclude: What my boss does and says makes me feel bad and switches me off. The quality of their performance is then directly linked to this answer. When they feel good, they are physically and mentally healthier. They have energy, think more clearly, use the vision as a beacon, make necessary changes to be accountable and support their colleagues.

Losing Control of the Wheel

I ran into George in the reception area recently. Carrying doughnuts and cookies, he said he was going into a meeting and these were for the team. I said something about how thoughtful this was and how glad his team would be.

"No," he said, "you've got it wrong. I am going to tell them they are performing so badly, we may as well spend a good time together before the ship sinks!"

George clearly does not "get it." What he was about to do would actually switch his team off even more. To give George his due, he probably believes this kind of message will energize the team and make things happen. He has no idea he has better behavioral options.

George has often said he's not interested in people's feelings – he's there to get a job done. What he doesn't get is that it's the feelings of his team that gets the job done … and these feelings are the direct consequence of his behaviors. This means, as a leader. George is responsible and accountable for learning how to behave in spirited ways to cultivate positive emotions in his team members.

GEORGE'S BEHAVIOR IS A LIABILITY

His behavior switches others off. He empties their emotional tanks. He reduces the human asset value of the organization.

George has a strong desire to succeed. Yet, he continues to sabotage himself and his team. He is trapped by ego beliefs that set off behaviors, causing others to disengage from him.

The Belief-Feeling-Behavior Wheel

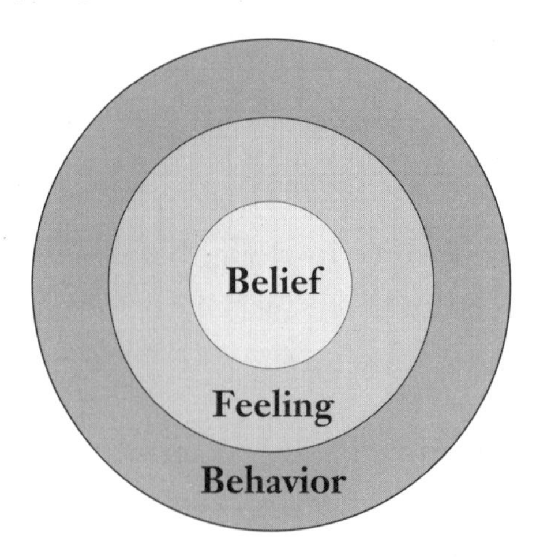

This is how it works. If you *believe* people enjoy your company and gravitate to you, then you will *feel* good around others. Your *behavior* will be inviting and people will enjoy being around you – which then confirms your belief that others like you. This belief becomes a self-fulfilling prophecy.

Take a look at the difference between George's ego beliefs and Dave's spirited beliefs and you will see why they behave so differently.

George's Beliefs:

- I am smarter than others
- I am right; they are wrong
- If it were not for them, I would be achieving more
- I'm OK. You're not OK.

Dave's Beliefs:

- I can achieve great things
- Others have skills and perspectives I do not have
- I need the abilities of others to achieve my goals
- I'm OK. You're OK.

Our ego wants to protect us. Its job is to make us feel good about ourselves, so it believes "I'm OK. You're not OK." This causes behaviors that turn others off.

George's behavior sends the message, "I have the knowledge, expertise and ideas, the solutions and strategic know-how. You do it my way. Don't rock the boat and everything will be fine."

Nothing is fine, though, because the team has no spirit!

THE EGO BELIEF-FEELING-BEHAVIOR WHEEL

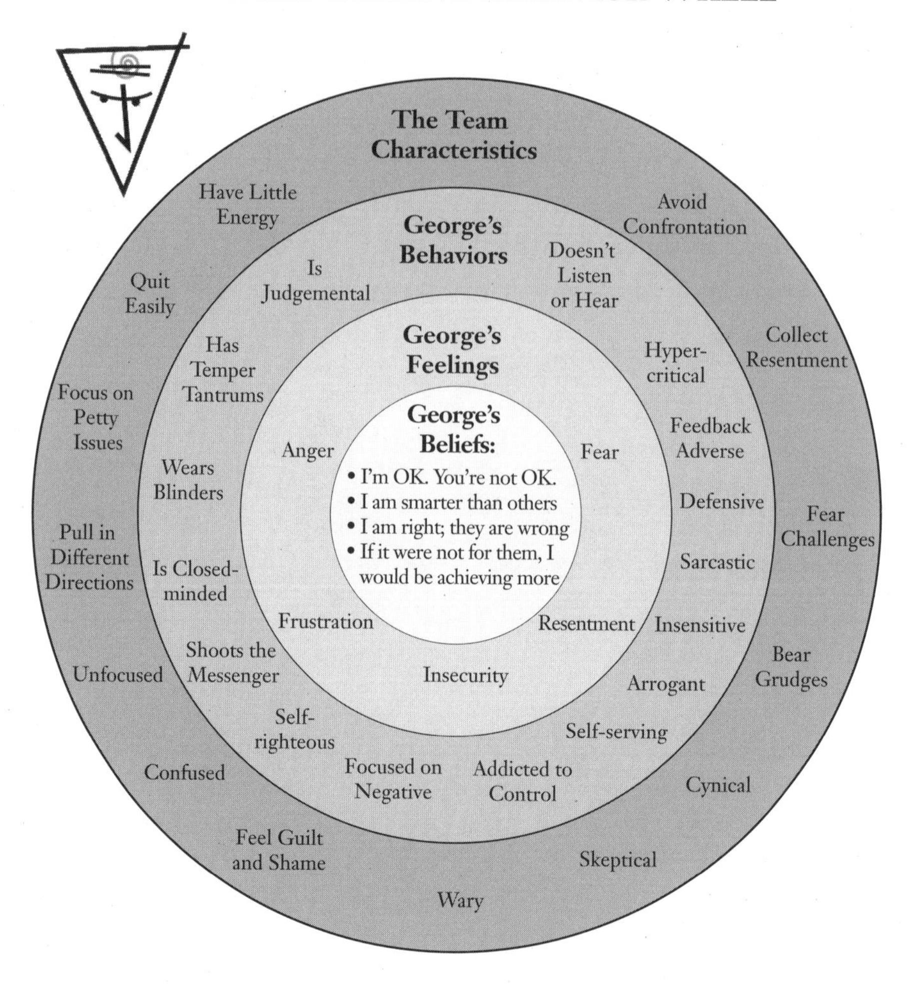

Actually, George feels very vulnerable and has a great fear of failure, but he hides this from himself and others. When faced with challenging situations, George becomes aggressive, has temper tantrums and behaves like a bully. He switches off his team, naming, shaming and blaming others, filling their tanks with low-octane fuel!

Being switched-off and tuned-out, his team is unable to take constructive action. As a result, they show little accountability and they perform poorly. This causes George's fear of failure to intensify, and his ego behaviors – in an effort to protect poor, hapless George – go from bad to worse. He says and does things that take his team's self-esteem down even further … and they, ultimately, fail.

*Who's in **Your** Driver's Seat?*
Clue #1: Check Your Ego Behaviors

Are you a leader whose behaviors switch others off?

To answer this question, use the Ego Belief-Feeling-Behavior Wheel to check the behaviors you use with the people who report to you.

This can be a challenging exercise because, if your ego is in the driver's seat, guess what? You will deny you have any of these behaviors. Only your spirit has the necessary courage to be honest and objective.

So, the question becomes: How can you put spirit in the driver's seat?

1. Think of the person in your team with whom you have the most difficult relationship and check the behaviors on the wheel as though you are that person. Look at yourself through that person's eyes.
2. If you find yourself saying, "Yes, but …," then try again because your ego has taken the driver's seat once more.
3. Serious about understanding your Spirit Equivalent? Then, make a copy of the Ego-Belief-Feeling-Behavior

Wheel for each of your team members and ask them to circle the behaviors they've seen you display. This option is pure spirit!

DAVE'S BEHAVIOR IS AN ASSET

His behavior switches others on. He fills their emotional tanks. He enhances the human asset value of the organization.

Dave has an interesting way of explaining synergy – he calls it the **1 + 1 = 3** concept. This means when two or more people get together, with spirit in the driver's seat, they create performance that goes beyond 1 + 1 = 2. Dave has seen it again and again. When people truly collaborate, the result is greater than the sum of their individual capabilities. So, when Dave walks into a meeting and looks around the table at his team, they see he believes in them and feels excited about what they have to offer. This fills their emotional tanks with premium fuel and powers them to success.

THE SPIRITED BELIEF-FEELING-BEHAVIOR WHEEL

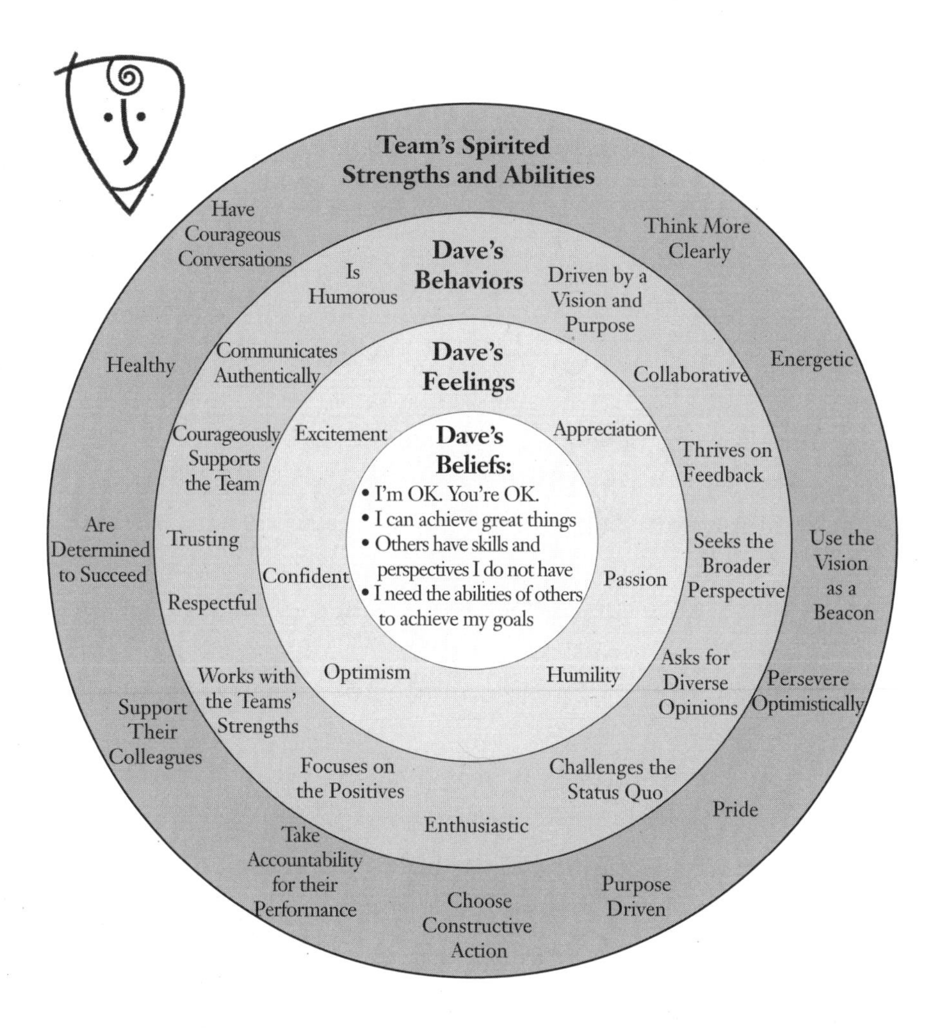

*Who's in **Your** Driver's Seat?*
Clue #2: Check Your Spirited Behavior

Mark the behaviors on the Spirited Belief-Feeling-Behavior Wheel that you use with the people who report to you.

WHO IS YOUR DOMINANT DRIVER?

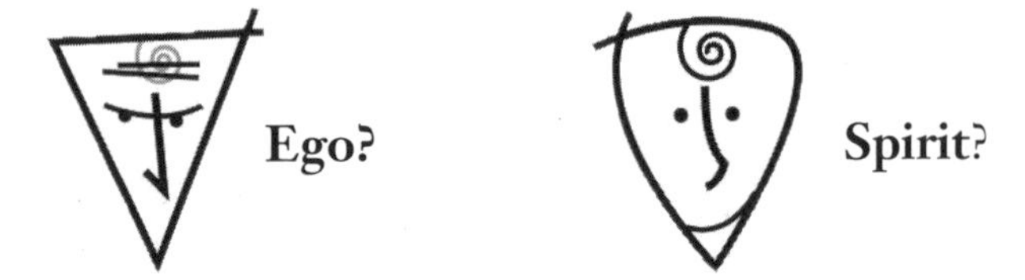

Total the number of behaviors you identified on the ego wheel and compare the total you have on the spirit wheel.

Your total for ego behaviors. ❒

Your total for spirit behaviors. ❒

Do you have more spirited behaviors? Or, more ego behaviors?

Are your behaviors switching others on or switching them off?

Are you in-spirit-ing them or dis-spirit-ing them? Creating inspiration or desperation? This is a seriously important question because the answer can mean the difference between your success and failure as a leader and the success or failure of your team … and your organization's strategy.

Now, let's discover the power of language to switch others on or off. Listen to the way George and Dave speak.

4

Firing On All Cylinders

Listen to Your Language

Winston Churchill said, "By swallowing evil words unsaid, no one has ever harmed his stomach."

Anytime a team comes together to achieve a goal, the words that pass between them – and how they are expressed – have a switch-on, switch-off effect. What we say and how we say it has huge consequences for accountability and performance. This makes language and how we use it an extremely powerful tool.

It all comes back to e-motion.

The first response we have to something someone says to us is always an emotional one. We will hear something that either creates a good feeling or a bad feeling within us. **It is this feeling that determines the quality of our performance.**

Here's what happens: Someone says something to us. We feel good or bad. Our energy level will adjust up or down, matching the feeling. The level of our energy dictates how we apply our intelligence and talent. Good feelings create high energy and high energy is spirit. Spirit has superior capabilities and intelligence, which assists us in delivering remarkable performance.

Bad feelings create low energy, which causes us to be dis-spirited. In this switched-off state, we will use limited amounts of our true capabilities and intelligence.

There are two kinds of leadership language – ego language and spirited language. The language we use will determine whether our team is:

- Misfiring and failing
- Firing on all cylinders and succeeding

LANGUAGE THAT CAUSES MISFIRING CYLINDERS

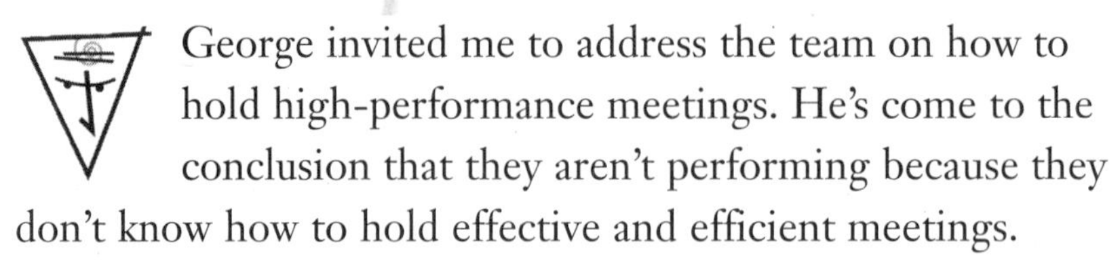

George invited me to address the team on how to hold high-performance meetings. He's come to the conclusion that they aren't performing because they don't know how to hold effective and efficient meetings.

I suspected this was George's ego self, putting the problem "out there" instead of taking spirited ownership of it himself … and by "out there" I mean finding something – or someone else – to blame.

As I watched this team in action, it became all too evident the problem was not poor meeting-management skills at all. The problem was, with ego in the driver's seat, George expressed himself in ways that switched off his team members. As they struggled to address the agenda, I saw how George's language caused his team members to resort to self-protection, denial, withdrawal and silence. They were so busy reacting to the things George's ego said, they became incapable of thinking clearly.

The agenda was forgotten as they began to focus on ego-related "small stuff." Eventually they were so switched off, they were just nodding their heads in agreement with whatever George said.

If George could be a fly on the wall and listen to himself speak, he could realize the very behaviors he wants his team to demonstrate are the very same behaviors his ego language crushes. He is totally unaware of how demeaning and patronizing his ego language sounds … and would probably be surprised to know how talented his team really is. The words and expressions he uses switches off their talent. I thought to myself, "This man could be a great leader if only he knew how to slide his spirited self into the driver's seat."

George's ego doesn't possess the kind of vocabulary that will fill his team with premium fuel. And, because he believes "my team doesn't get it. I have to push, pull, prod, coerce, direct and control them," he's frustrated. He then says things that make him sound self-righteous, hyper-critical and judgmental of everyone but himself. His words create feelings of embarrassment, shame, guilt, despair, fear and confusion.

When we put spirit in the passenger seat and allow ego to drive, we automatically have ego conversations, ego meetings and ego discussions where the underlying message is always loud and clear: I'm OK. You're not!

Let's listen to how George's language causes misfiring cylinders and sets his team up for mediocre performance:

Watch Your Language!

When leaders with large egos become frustrated they often explode and become accusatory. This is when George will say something that sounds like, "I don't believe this! Did you not hear a single thing I said?" Some of his favorite expressions are, "*What on earth gave you the idea you could do it that way?*" and, "*Which of my instructions did you not understand?*" Or perhaps he will shout, "*No! No! No! Let me remind you we are on the line to deliver in two days! Do you mind telling me how you intend to pull this off?*"

There are times when George's ego becomes passive-aggressive and expresses a veiled insult. Here are two examples of his pet expressions: "*With all due respect to Joe* (here comes the put-down...) *he is completely incorrect in his assumption*" and, "*No offense intended* (here comes the put-down...) *but what you just recommended is totally ridiculous!*"

Ego has a habit of saying things indirectly rather than being open and honest. This often involves burying the real message in a joke or using sarcasm as a way of telling someone something. Here are some of George's ulterior expressions: "*James here loves to spend lots of time with the ladies in the office. He's not so crazy about work though. Just joking, pal.*"

When a team member is late, George says, *"Hello Samantha! Guess your watch is on Pacific time?"*

George's ego is not good at listening to other perspectives, either. He will pretend to listen and then cut the person short with a *"Yes, but ..." "I understand that is your opinion, but ..." "I hear you, but ...."* Very often George will ask the team for input, appear to listen for a while, and then he'll make an autocratic decision based on what he wants to do: *"Okay, team, I heard what you've said. Now, here's what's going to happen."* This leaves the team wondering why he actually bothered to ask them for their ideas at all.

LOW-OCTANE RESPONSES

So what can employees/team members actually say when the boss uses ego language? What options are available to them?

That's what I saw happening in George's meeting. The more he used ego language, the more his team resorted to "low-octane" responses, such as silence, withdrawing something they had said, rephrasing a statement so that George would not be offended and offering "vanilla" responses. I heard his team use expressions such as, *"That's not exactly what I meant"* (when it was exactly what he meant, originally), *"Let me say it another way"* (meaning, "Let me say it your way, George"), *"I'm not suggesting that"* (when she actually was) and the favorite don't-make-waves response – *"I guess you're right."*

FIRING ON ALL CYLINDERS

I called Dave today to set up that coffee date he suggested on our previous call. "I'm glad you called," he said. "We're having a meeting to celebrate our quarterly results and to consolidate plans for the next quarter. Would you facilitate a brainstorm for us? Then, maybe we could have our coffee date after that."

So on a sunny day in Texas, I found myself observing Dave and his team in action ... and, as you may have already guessed, the difference between this meeting and George's meeting was astounding.

The team members assertively expressed different opinions and feelings. Each person presented a strong argument to motivate his point of view. They all were well-informed, quoting statistics and innovative trends they had gleaned from the latest literature and conferences they recently attended. They referred to, and included, feedback and information they received from staff members not present. The spirited discussion was punctuated by body language that was clearly in harmony with what was being said. The energy in the room was invigorating.

Dave started the meeting by saying, "*Remember, as always, I want you to argue with me. I need you to challenge my viewpoint. I'm interested in every possible way of seeing this opportunity, so, let's get started – and remember – keep an open mind.*"

Once Dave had set the meeting up, his team members responded, using the language of challenge and feedback, saying, "*I have another take on this.*" "*I'm going to push back on that.*" "*Are you open to some feedback?*"

The team made repeated reference to their shared vision and their commitment to this with statements like, "*We have a great vision, let's make it happen.*" "*Speak to me about how that aligns with our vision."* I noticed this team talked about "*when*" and not "*if*."

During the brainstorm process, they would get ideas going by saying, "*Let me paint a picture.*" "*Let's play the 'what if' game.*" "*What if anything were possible and we had no restrictions?*" "*Let's challenge our perspective.*"

Dave and his team spoke about "*demonstrating the company values.*" Their sense of urgency was punctuated by phrases like, "*We've got no time to waste. The competitors are snapping at our heels.*"

The language of collaboration was loud and clearly expressed in phrases like, "*Let's put our heads together on this.*" "*What do you need from me?*" "*I suggest we have an inter-departmental meeting to plan this.*" "*I can let you have some resources for this.*" There was very little use of the word, "*you.*" Instead, Dave and his team used "*us*" and "*we.*"

Action steps and timelines were developed. The team agreed on how to communicate their decisions to the staff. They congratulated each other on an excellent meeting ... and they finished on time!

It occurred to me that every person in the room had participated and without having to be asked. Dave closed the meeting with spirited words of encouragement and trust, saying, "*We can do this! I have full confidence in your ability to make this happen! You've come through in the past. I know you can do it again.*"

I left the meeting aware of the energizing sense of purpose and confidence that Dave's spirited language had created. With his spirited self in the driver's seat, Dave spontaneously has spirited conversations, spirited meetings and spirited discussions. The way in which he expresses his expectations, requirements, ideas, plans, goals, and needs gets the team firing on all cylinders. His language is open, honest, clear, and informative, every word designed to foster collaboration … and Dave's words inspire (in-spirit) the team, filling their emotional tanks with pride, hope, courage and purpose.

The Language You Use

Are your team members firing on all cylinders? Do you have spirited conversations? Spirited meetings? Spirited discussions?

You can discover the answer to this question by listening to your team and your work force because spirited conversations trigger spirited responses from others. If your employees speak with confidence, courage, enthusiasm, ambition and single-mindedness about achieving the agreed-upon goals – together, then this means that the leaders are using spirited language.

When we speak spirited language, so will our teams, which is one of the reasons they produce extraordinary results.

*Who's in **Your** Driver's Seat?*
Clue #3: Check Your Language

If putting spirit in the driver's seat is important to you as a leader, start practicing awareness.

In Chapter 4, behavioral clues were offered to help you become aware of how your ego self behaves. In this chapter, language clues will help you recognize how your ego self speaks. Replacing the language of ego with spirited language is one way of putting spirit in the driver's seat.

At first the ego will try very hard to stay in the driver's seat. However, once we begin to enjoy the success that spirited language brings, it becomes easier and easier to make the ego a passenger. It's all about making a conscious choice to designate spirit as your driver.

In the next chapter, there's an easy 3-step process, showing you how to be in charge of who is in your driver's seat.

5

CHOOSING THE DESIGNATED DRIVER

Take the Ego Test

The results of George's next annual employee survey were a disaster.

Although he was a brilliant marketer, well-connected and closed many big deals, Fred – his boss – could no longer overlook the fact that George's team was extremely dissatisfied and unhappy. They complained that George's behaviors were contrary to the culture and values of the organization. He seemed to be unable to live the company's values, particularly those of Team Spirit, Collaboration and Employee Growth and Development.

Fred had been reading about how former GE CEO, Jack Welch, concluded he would rather retain a leader who practiced the values but didn't deliver results than someone who delivered results but didn't embrace the values. Welch realized it is possible to train someone in their job skills, but it's extremely difficult to train someone to lead with values and engage others.

Much to George's surprise, he was fired.

At the exit interview, his boss offered him confronting feedback about the effect his ego had on his team. George discounted this feedback, thinking that his team just wanted him fired. Ten days later, his son's teacher called George to set up a meeting. Jake had written an essay and she was concerned about the content. In his essay, George's son had written about wishing his dad would believe he was a good kid, a special kid, a smart kid … and he just wanted his dad to stop telling him how he was messing up and what he could do better.

This was the turning point for George. Suddenly everything his boss had said began ringing in his ears. For the first time, George understood his ego needed to shift into the passenger seat.

If you watch George in action in his new position, you would be amazed. Months of coaching and hard work on his part have taught him how to put his spirited self in the driver's seat. Now, George tells anyone who will listen about the tyranny of the ego and how it is truly possible to put your ego in the passenger seat.

Dave? He's being groomed for a vice president's position and it wouldn't surprise anyone if, one day in the not too distant future, Dave becomes CEO.

Putting the Ego in the Passenger Seat

Like most things in life, making the right choice about anything has its foundation in awareness. In the workplace, where much of what we say and do has a lasting effect, it's important we are aware of our behaviors and our words.

Without this awareness, we'll become trapped by the tyranny of the ego, not realizing the havoc it can create. Because of this, it's vital for leaders to understand the concept of who is in the driver's seat. When they are driven by the ego, they can cause great damage to themselves, the people they work with and the organizations they work for.

Think about how much more productive and successful leaders and their teams could be if they had the skills to put spirit back in the workplace.

So, what if you had a quick and easy way to decide who is in your driver's seat? You could be sitting in a meeting that's not going the way you would like it. You could be planning for a difficult phone call. You could be preparing a speech. Perhaps someone has said something upsetting to you, or you may be preparing to confront your boss … and you want to be sure your ego is not going to do and say things that get in the way of you achieving your objectives.

Imagine how useful it would be to be able to quickly identify who's in the driver's seat. Then, if you decided you wanted to change the designated driver, you could make the shift and choose spirited behavior and language, all in a matter of minutes.

This skill will give you the power to easily achieve any desired outcome in any situation. Imagine that!

PUTTING THE SPIRITED SELF IN THE DRIVER'S SEAT – THE 3-STEP PROCESS:

1. First, take the Ego Test

2. Second, choose spirited behaviors and spirited language.

3. Third, take the ego antidote. Then add a dose of humility.

1. TAKE THE EGO TEST

At all times, be aware of what you are thinking and feeling and the physical sensations in your body. If you're thinking negative thoughts or feeling tense about a situation, person or event, stop and take this 1-minute **Ego Test**. It will quickly and easily tell you if your ego is in the driver's seat and give you the opportunity to make the shift to spirit.

The Ego Test

Check the indicators that apply to you:

- ❑ You are emotionally charged up about an event or a person.

- ❑ You are rationalizing, intellectualizing and/or justifying.

- ❑ You are using negative words or labels to describe yourself or others.

- ❑ You have developed a physical symptom – headache, backache, muscular pain, flu, lethargy, stomach pain, diarrhea or other physical problem.

- ❑ You are tense and have lost your sense of humor.

❑ You feel unfocused and your thinking has become cloudy.

❑ You think about a person or an incident over and over again.

❑ **Your Score**

A score of zero indicates your spirited self is in the driver's seat. You will not need to proceed to the following two steps. A check before any of the characteristics on the 7-point Ego Test indicates your ego is the driver. The higher the number of checks, the greater the control of the ego.

If your ego is driving, it is important for you to take a deep breath and *actually write or say – aloud – to yourself*, **"My ego is in the driver's seat. I need to make a switch."** Doing this allows you to take ownership of the results of the ego test and then consciously and purposefully make the choice to put spirit in the driver's seat. It also gives you some time to collect your thoughts and move into a spirited mode.

This Ego Test list may surprise you, because you haven't thought of these seven conditions as being signs of ego. Perhaps you believe this is just the way we are when we are stressed or challenged. *The truth is, when the spirited self is in the driver's seat, we don't demonstrate any of the above seven signs.* Why? Because the spirited self doesn't feel like it has to compete with others. It doesn't compare itself to others and doesn't judge itself or others.

What the spirited self does, instead, is humbly keep an open mind, listen to all points of view and come to balanced conclusions. It operates on the principle of flow, not fight or flight.

2. CHOOSE SPIRITED BEHAVIORS AND SPIRITED LANGUAGE

Your spirit will be firmly in the driver's seat the moment you stop rationalizing, intellectualizing, justifying, accusing, being defensive, criticizing, judging, complaining and blaming others. Then, instead, start asking questions, reflect back what you are hearing and show genuine curiosity, interest and concern.

Decide what you want to achieve and identify the spirited behavioral options you have available to you (see the Behavior Wheel). Decide how your spirited self would express itself differently. Then, select words and grammar the spirited self would use to convey the message (see some of the ways Dave expressed himself). Finally, make the necessary behavioral and language adjustments.

3. FOR STUBBORN EGOS, TAKE THE EGO ANTIDOTE – ADD A DOSE OF HUMILITY

In Step 1, you take ownership of the fact your ego is driving you and no happy endings are on the horizon. This should put a stop to any rationalizing. However, there are times when we really are charged by a person or event and find it tough to shift the ego. That's when it's important to remember the ego is self-righteous and will not give up the driver's seat easily. Also keep in mind, while the ego is driving, we cannot reach balanced conclusions, and our perspectives will be biased and lopsided.

If you find that your ego does not want to shift seats, use this powerful exercise to **neutralize self-righteousness and replace it with humility.**

The feeling of true humility can disempower the ego. Humility is the understanding that we are just like everyone else – no better, no worse. This negates the ego's primary purpose, which is to fool us into believing we are better than others. Here's how we add a dose of humility:

If you spot it, you've got it.*

Think of the person, situation or event you are emotionally charged about. Write down three negative words or short phrases you would use to describe this person or situation. Now take each word or phrase and apply it to yourself. Next, ask yourself two questions:

1. In what situations does this word or label apply to me?
2. To whom am I doing exactly what I am accusing the other(s) of?

You will discover somewhere, in some situation, with some other person, right now in your life, the words you wrote down also apply to you. Accept the fact you possess the very same characteristics you have used to negatively describe others or a situation.

This exercise is called, "**If you spot it, you've got it**" because, if you are honest with yourself, you will discover what you see in others are the identical qualities you refuse to see in yourself. The humility you feel when you realize you are no better (or worse) than anyone else, will provide the push you need to shift the ego into the passenger seat. Now you are ready for Step 3.

**This is a remarkable exercise that I learned from my brilliant mentor, Dr. John Demartini.*

KEEPING YOURSELF TUNED

The ability to catch your ego in action and deliberately shift from ego to spirit will improve over time. However, we should never underestimate the ego and its desire to be the driver. This is why it is important to keep yourself tuned. Be present at all times, stay alert and aware, notice how you are feeling, watch your behaviors and listen to your words. You will quickly become adept at knowing when you are slipping back into ego. Apply a strong dose of humility with, "If you spot it, you've got it," and choose spirited behaviors and language.

This is a lifelong journey because the ego will never leave us. Actually the ego is a friend. We are constantly reminded we have a choice to let our spirited self drive by watching the crises the ego creates.

THE RIGHT TO CHOOSE

At some point in our lives, we will either choose to acknowledge the tyranny of the ego, as George did, or choose not to acknowledge this, preferring to remain unaware and allow the ego to stay in the driver's seat. This is a personal choice, and every individual has the right to make it.

What leaders do not have the right to do, however, is to control, hurt, suppress and damage others because of the emotional immaturity, insensitivity, lack of awareness and often destructive interpersonal behaviors of their egos.

Most people will not have to look far to see how executives and other leaders who have ego in the driver's seat negatively impact the performance of their employees. If you're one of the fortunate ones who work with a leader who has the spirited self in the driver's seat, you know how personally and professionally inspiring this is.

SECTION 3

Making Spirited Decisions

6

Spirited Decisions from Boardroom to Backroom

Taking Ego Out of the Equation

In Sections 1 and 2, we learned the first step of spirited leadership is to liberate the spirit of the team by connecting with the members in e-motion-ally positive ways – by switching them onto the vision and goals and in-spirit-ing them for the journey of getting from where they are to where they want to be.

In order to offer superior performance, teams will need to apply superior intelligence so they can make the best strategic and tactical decisions along the way.

Leaders at all levels are making decisions, large and small. Collectively, these decisions will move the company forward, keep it in neutral or move it backward.

The trick is to get leaders – throughout the organization – to make aligned decisions from boardroom to backroom, keeping the company moving in the agreed-upon direction. For this to happen, leaders at all levels will need to have spirit in the driver's seat. Why? Because only spirited leaders are able to lay their personal agendas aside.

Spirited decision-makers are driven by the organization's vision and strategies and will make decisions that will support the corporate goals. As you may have witnessed, ego-driven decision-makers make defensive, short-term, self-serving and inappropriate decisions, regardless of whether it's right or wrong for the company – strategically aligned or not.

Just as there are two types of leadership behaviors and languages, so there are two types of decisions in business – ego decisions and spirited decisions.

Ego decisions are poor decisions because they are based on limited use of intelligence, limited attention to the real facts and a distorted view of the emotional issues. Ego-driven leaders make decisions using half their intelligence, half the facts and half the story.

Spirited decisions are intelligent decisions. With spirit in the driver's seat, leaders and their teams are released from the petty ego issues and are, as a result, free to tap into their highest intelligence, SQ, to explore the full facts and discover the whole story. The decisions they make are objective and enlightened.

The Ego Mind Uses Limited Intelligence

Our brains have three intelligences: IQ, EQ and SQ. These three provide us with three different ways of thinking and three different kinds of information.

Ego causes us to focus on ourselves and use far less IQ and EQ than we are actually capable of and, in some cases, we will even have a preference for only one intelligence, which is usually IQ. In addition, without spirit in the driver's seat, we cannot access SQ, so with limited amounts of IQ and EQ – and zero SQ – we become so narrow-minded that *we are literally using less of our minds.*

Without SQ, we don't have the capacity to challenge our own assumptions, to see the panoramic view, to take the long-term risks, and to make inspired (in-spirited) decisions. Only SQ enables us to break free of our hard-wired thinking.

While the spirit mind is clear, focused, curious and leading edge, the ego mind is scattered, troubled, confused and tired. **With ego in the driver's seat, our genius is in the passenger seat.**

George's Outdated Roadmap

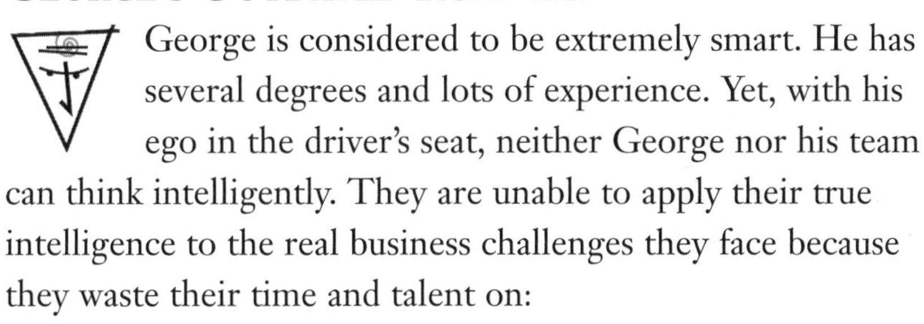

George is considered to be extremely smart. He has several degrees and lots of experience. Yet, with his ego in the driver's seat, neither George nor his team can think intelligently. They are unable to apply their true intelligence to the real business challenges they face because they waste their time and talent on:

1. Being defensive.

2. Avoiding uncomfortable situations.

3. Trying to squelch the bad feelings they experience.
4. Hiding how vulnerable they really feel.

Intellectually, this is crippling … to the point they become distracted and unfocused in their thinking and make poor decisions. Not because they are not smart, educated or experienced but because their thinking is affected by their negative emotions, which has caused them to tune out. As leader, George's ego has set this effect in motion:

Switched-off emotions

↓

Switched-off intelligence

In addition, as we've seen in previous chapters, George's ego doesn't like dialogue, confrontation or debate. This means his plans and decisions are based on the **half of the story** his ego wants to hear and the **half of the facts** his ego prefers to know. This gives him a lopsided perspective based on lopsided perceptions which, in turn, cause him to make lopsided decisions and operate with an outdated roadmap.

Without inviting, hearing and including the team's input, the aspects of the story he did not hear and the facts he did not include in his planning will always come back to bite him. Then, as usual, he'll blame the team.

EGO-THINKING EQUATION

The multiplicative effect of ego thinking is best illustrated by this equation:

$$\frac{1}{2} \times \frac{1}{2} = \frac{1}{4}$$

½ the story x ½ the facts = ¼ the performance

With his team's intelligence disengaged, George's plans, decisions and execution can only be a quarter as successful as they could, otherwise, be. With limited amounts of IQ and EQ and no SQ, the chances of George's team making profitable, growth-oriented, future-focused decisions and putting them into action are minimal. Instead, they will continue to make un-in-spirit-ed decisions and deliver un-in-spirit-ed, mediocre performance.

Here's a perfect example of ½ **x** ½ = ¼ thinking: Coca-Cola missed some of the most important beverage trends in the past 20 years. They were late going into fruit-flavored teas. Snapple did it first. Coke was late going into sports drinks. Gatorade was first. Then, Coke was late going into designer water. Nestle is number one in the world. Coke also was late getting into New Age beverages and is still trying to catch up with Red Bull.

We can only assume if the decision-makers at Coca-Cola were open to exploring the whole story and all the facts – with an open mind – they would have become aware of these immense opportunities sooner. Instead, they became prisoners of their limited ego mind. They had the same information as their competitors, yet they were unable to think beyond their ego.

The story of Ken Kuturagi is another prime example of how leaders can function with half the facts and half the story. Sony's single most profitable business, Play Station, was invented by Ken Kuturagi, who found little support inside the company for this invention and had to fight the system for years. The egos of his leaders prevented them from seeing the broader view and recognizing the brilliance of this product.

Eventually Kuturagi found a senior executive who could rise above his ego and access SQ – the head of Sony Music in Japan. We all know the rest of the story.

DAVE'S LATEST AND GREATEST ROADMAP

Let me paint the scene. Dave's spirited leadership style has rubbed off on his team. They are e-motion-ally tanked up and geared for success. As Dave likes to tell them, "Now that we're all fired up, the next step is to develop the most excellent roadmap possible and drive intelligently in order to reach our destination without being involved in an accident or taking any time-consuming and unnecessary detours. For this we need the full facts and the whole story. So let's go to it!" In this scenario, Dave is working his formula that:

Switched-on emotions

↓

Switched-on intelligence

SWITCHED-ON TEAMS ARE INTELLIGENT TEAMS

Spirited teams are intelligent teams, not because they have more academic degrees or more years of better experience. No, it's because they utilize their brainpower – they literally use more IQ, EQ and SQ than ego-driven teams. Being highly intelligent is easy for spirited teams because they are not "sweating the small stuff." And their minds are open to the broader view.

Let's learn from Dave again. Remember the meeting Dave asked me to attend? As I watched him in action, I saw how he encouraged the team to explore the whole story, analyze the full facts and then take that information to the next level with SQ.

He mobilized their IQ by leading with questions, questions and then more questions, pushing for as many additional facts as he could get by saying things like, "*That's not enough. Tell me more.*" "*Okay, what's missing?*" "*Have we consulted the leaders in the field?*"

He mobilized their EQ by asking qualitative questions like: "*Okay, tell me the story with a beginning, middle and end.*" "*What's going on with the other folks in the situation? What are they feeling, needing, expecting?*" "*What are we doing to switch them off?*" "*How can we engage them in the process?*"

Dave listened carefully and made notes. He deliberately sought out others who had different opinions – "*Joe, I know you have a totally different take on this – take me through it.*" "*Okay, anyone with another viewpoint?*"

Then he would blend the different points of view and combine different realities – "*This is good stuff! Let's look at how we can combine Joe's idea with Susan's concept and see if we can come up with something we can use.*"

Finally, he pulled the information together by using a "what if" scenario as a way of synthesizing the information the team had compiled.

Dave then mobilized the SQ of the team by instructing them as follows: "Team, we've done a great job, collecting all the facts and understanding the whole story, but that's not enough.

What we do with this information is crucial to our success, so now, let's take it to the next level and look at it through a different lens."

"Here's how it works," Dave continued. "In order to make powerful decisions, you need to grasp the concept of **1 + 1 = 3**. If we use this information to make 1 + 1 = 2, this means we're still prisoners of yesterday's way of thinking.

"Let me give you some examples of what I mean:

"Swatch®, a popular, U.S. watchmaker, is a great example of 1 + 1 = 3. They were getting slam-dunked in the market by their Japanese competitors and had to do something different. They could have analyzed the facts and the industry story and made 1 + 1 = 2 by making improvements to design and quality. Instead, they used SQ. They combined Swiss watch-making skills with Italian fashion design and then borrowed plastic engineering skills from LEGO®. The result was exceptional growth and revenue.

"Only 1 + 1 = 3 thinking could have assisted them in deciding on this unique combination. This means they were able to take the full facts and the whole story to the next level. Neat, huh?"

The team was listening with rapt attention as Dave shared another example. "The way Starbucks thinks about coffee is an example of 1 + 1 = 3. They take great coffee beans and combine this with a special customer experience – a place to hang out, sit on couches, read books, connect to the Internet, make personalized music CDs and have business meetings. The result? Millions of people are prepared to pay $3.50 for a latte. The consumer did not ask for this new coffee experience. Instead, Starbucks strategists were able to see beyond the norm and discover the consumer's deeper, unexpressed needs. This is SQ thinking."

Dave's team members started to get where he was going. One team member, Jeff, offered the example of how Southwest Airlines used SQ when they reinvented the ticketing and routing methods. "By adopting a point-to-point routing system, Southwest keeps its jets in the air for 2 or 3 hours more than most other airlines, thereby using its capital more efficiently," he explained. "The result? Southwest, which is still a young company, now has a market value greater than the next five airlines combined."

Mark added, "Dell is another example of 1 + 1 = 3 thinking."

"And so is Apple," Shirley added. "They hired Jonathon Ive, a young British designer who reinvented the ugly PC into the jazzy work of art – the first iMac. Look at how this has changed customer expectations! Apple keeps raising the bar on what people expect to see in a PC. I guess this kind of radical innovation at the product level requires SQ thinking."

"Okay," Dave said. "Now let's apply this to the information we have. Let's look at this through fresh eyes. Forget about the bigger picture! Go beyond this room, beyond this building, this organization, this industry, this state, this country – and tell me what you see that will impact us. Ask the stupid questions no one else has asked. Convert this into possibilities others cannot see. Look for opportunities in unusual places."

That day, Dave and his team came up with the germ of an idea that eventually earned the company millions of dollars – with great kudos for them – plus hefty bonuses!

SECTION 4

Creating Spirited Accountability

7

Enjoying the Journey

Letting Go

One afternoon Harry went mountain climbing. Things were going very well. Then suddenly the path he was walking on gave way, taking Harry with it. Harry managed to grab a small branch on the side of the mountain. Holding on for dear life, he screamed, "Help! Help! Is anybody up there?"

Miraculously, the clouds parted and a beam of light illuminated Harry as he hung from the branch. A voice – clearly the voice of God – spoke directly to Harry and said, "Harry, I will save you. I am all that is good, all that is true and all that has meaning. Let go, Harry. I will save you. Let go."

Harry thought long and hard about this. Then, with a sudden burst of conviction, he looked up the mountain and shouted, "Is anybody else up there?"

When the ego self is in the driver's seat, we find it difficult to let go and trust in the abilities of others. So how do we hold others accountable?

Let's review the spirited delegation and accountability scenario:

The team is e-motion-ally and intellectually engaged, their tanks are filled with premium fuel, they are firing on all cylinders, they have the newest roadmap available, they are revving the engine and awaiting their leader to give them final instructions. The leader delegates the tasks and gets out of the way as they engage first gear, press the accelerator and go.

Then there is the ego scenario:

The team is e-motion-ally and intellectually disengaged, their tanks are half-filled with low-octane fuel, they have an outdated roadmap and, due to the misfiring cylinders, the team is sitting in the car, but the car will not start – so delegation and accountability become a futile exercise.

The Backseat Driver or The Team Coach Enjoying The Ride?

Delegating accountability means you are not going to do it … someone else is. Letting go to others requires courage and faith in the abilities of others. Unfortunately, ego leaders have neither faith in others nor the courage to let go. Instead, they are motivated by fear, and this sets up a chain reaction that backfires on them:

- ♦ They switch the team off emotionally.
- ♦ This disables the team intellectually.
- ♦ The dis-spirited team lets things fall through the cracks.
- ♦ The leader is fearful that his team will let him down.
- ♦ The anxious leader becomes a backseat driver.
- ♦ This prevents the team from taking personal accountability.
- ♦ The leader then confronts them in true ego style.
- ♦ They all throw accountability "over the wall."
- ♦ The results are poor or, at best, mediocre.

Ego-driven leaders continually look over the shoulders of their team and repeatedly grab the wheel to make a course correction rather than trusting that the team knows where they are going and how they will get there. It's understandable they would need to be backseat drivers, because their ego has not been able to lay the foundation for true accountability.

In the process, they disable their team and then are afraid to delegate to a group of dis-spirited people. And so they should be! A dis-spirited team is incapable of having the focus, purpose and commitment that will drive them to take accountability for delivering results.

Seeing this lack of accountability, the leader's ego behaviors and ego language come out in full force, switching the team off even further … and so the vicious cycle continues.

Spirited leaders, on the other hand, unlock the confidence, self-esteem and intellect of their teams and then focus the energy and commitment this creates on the key business outcomes. They give their teams the resources and tools needed to get the job done. They then delegate clearly and get out of the way, giving their teams credit for knowing how to do their jobs – and freedom to take accountability.

What about you? Are you an insecure backseat driver or are you the team coach enjoying the ride? Your answer will give you a clue about who's in your driver's seat.

Your Team Is a Reflection of You

The more spirited you are as a leader, the more accountable your team will be. Only switched-on teams are capable of true accountability.

The first step to building an engaged and accountable, high-performing team is to **take a reality check** and discover to what extent you are displaying spirited leadership. You are the leader of others – if you are spirited and switched on, they will be spirited and switched on. The reverse is also applicable here.

The team is a reflection of you … and you are a reflection of the person you report to. You can also apply this checklist to your boss. Is your boss a spirited leader or a leader with ego in the driver's seat?

The Spirited Leadership Checklist

Unenthusiastic	1 2 3 4 5	Enthusiastic
Pessimistic	1 2 3 4 5	Optimistic
Lethargic	1 2 3 4 5	Energized
Low determination	1 2 3 4 5	Determined
Fearful	1 2 3 4 5	Courageous
Lacking self confidence	1 2 3 4 5	Self-confident
Suspicious	1 2 3 4 5	Trusting
Clings to a narrow view	1 2 3 4 5	Seeks a broader view
Judgmental	1 2 3 4 5	Non-judgmental
Closed-minded	1 2 3 4 5	Open-minded
Skeptical, cynical	1 2 3 4 5	Unbiased, open
Arrogant	1 2 3 4 5	Humble
Hyper-critical	1 2 3 4 5	Builds others up
Bears grudges	1 2 3 4 5	Resolves issues
Self-serving	1 2 3 4 5	Seek common goals
No sense of humor	1 2 3 4 5	Good sense of humor
Dislikes feedback	1 2 3 4 5	Seeks feedback
Has health issues	1 2 3 4 5	Is healthy
Not goal-driven	1 2 3 4 5	Goal-driven
Sense of entitlement	1 2 3 4 5	Gratitude/appreciation

❐ **Total Score**

How do you rate?

What story does this checklist tell about you as leader? If you scored between 80-100, your spirit is in the driver's seat 80 percent to 100 percent of the time. Congratulations!

If you score 60-80, your spirited self is growing in strength, but there could still be four out of 10 situations in which your ego takes the driver's seat. These are four lost opportunities for making something positive happen!

Below 60? Your ego is in the driver's seat too often, which means on those occasions, you and your team are dealing with petty ego issues that will affect your ability to deliver exceptional results.

The ideal is to have as many scores of 4 and 5 as possible. **The higher your score, the higher the level of accountability in your team – and the more remarkable the results.**

Notice the characteristics in which you scored below 4. By completing this checklist, you've identified a wonderful opportunity. Apply the spirited leadership skills from the previous chapters and you will notice a measurable change in your ability as a leader to inspire your team to greatness.

There is, of course, one **disclaimer**. If your ego is in the driver's seat when you complete this checklist, the results will be of no value to you. So how will you know if your ego completed the checklist? Take the Ego Test back on page 56 again. Notice how you feel. Do you feel irritated, annoyed or skeptical? If you begin rationalizing and intellectualizing or if you withdraw, shut down, feel defensive and feel the need to ridicule the checklist, your ego is in the driver's seat. This means the results are not valid.

In order to put spirit in the driver's seat and obtain authentic results, you have two options: Take a dose of humility, using the "If you spot it, you've got it" exercise. For example, if you called the list "silly, dumb, or ridiculous," ask yourself, "How do these labels fit me?" You are sure to find, somewhere with someone in your life, you are currently being silly, dumb and ridiculous.

The second and most spirited option of all would be to ask others who will give you honest feedback to complete the Spirited Leadership Checklist for you.

My Spirited Driver's License

Please be aware ... this exercise is based on the fact that, to a greater or lesser degree, *every one of us* has the ego in the driver's seat – *every one of us displays ego behavior and uses ego language*. The goal is for this to happen on a few occasions as opposed to being a way of life.

Depending on the amount of time your ego is in the driver's seat, this charter may be either a minor or a major challenge, requiring minor adjustments or major changes:

Step 1

I, _______________ as executive/director/manager/supervisor of the _______________ team, undertake to enhance my team's ability to be accountable and deliver results by:

Creating a spirited team:

❒ Empowering my team emotionally

❒ Enabling my team intellectually

I will do this by:

1. Changing the following ego behaviors I have identified in myself:

____

____

____

____

____

I will replace these ego behaviors with the following spirited behaviors:

____

____

____

____

____

2. Changing the following ego language and expressions that I have identified in the way I speak:

____

____

____

____

____

I will replace this ego language with spirited language such as:

____

____

____

____

____

Signed: ____________________

Date: ______________________

Congratulations!

Call a meeting to tell your team they will be seeing several changes in your behavior. Explain what these changes will be. Wrap this explanation around a story of your choosing. This is an important step because, without doing this, the team will be suspicious of your motives and confused by your new behaviors, which will have a further negative impact on their performance. Be sure to use the new behaviors and language you identified in your charter during this meeting.

Then, track your team's performance over a period of three months. You will be astonished by the significant improvement in their performance measures.

8

Key Points

The theme of this book is that switched-on people produce switched-on results. Switched-off people produce switched-off results. When we are emotionally switched on, we will feel positive emotions – like determination, exhilaration, optimism and courage. These characteristics are a sign of having spirit in the driver's seat. When we work with spirit, we have enhanced capabilities that significantly increase the successful achievement of the key business outcomes.

There is a direct relationship between leadership's ability to switch on their teams and enhanced profitability and return on investment. For organizations, large and small, the degree to which each person can offer performance that contributes to superior results is a function of the quality of commitment and excitement the individual feels – and this is a function of being switched on and spirited.

Ultimately, having a spirited work force represents the competitiveness of the business.

ENHANCED ORGANIZATIONAL EFFECTIVENESS AND REVENUE THROUGH SPIRIT

Spirit is not a soft, esoteric issue. Putting spirit in the driver's seat is a core business imperative. This also makes it a core leadership imperative.

The good news is that being a spirited leader can come naturally to us. Why? Because we all have spirit. It is simply a matter of reconnecting with what we already possess but have forgotten to use. The way we reconnect with our spirited self is by becoming aware when our ego is in the driver's seat. At first you can use the 1-minute Ego Test. Soon you won't need the Ego Test at all because your body and your feelings will tell you immediately when your ego is driving.

Then, we shift the spirit into the driver's seat by choosing spirited behaviors and spirited language. If your ego is still clinging to the driver's seat, apply the ego antidote, "If you spot it, you've got it."

Spirit has three fundamental and measurable capabilities. Each of these includes several business strengths and skills that generate enhanced revenue.

1. The ability to be connected to one's true self

The business benefit (expressed as the leader and/or team member):

- I feel comfortable being authentically me.
- I have a clear purpose that is my driving force.
- My work has meaning.
- I am physically and mentally alert and healthy.
- I feel confident, energized, focused and committed.
- I express my requirements and expectations clearly.
- I take responsibility and accountability.
- My talent is revving at the highest level, I am firing on all cylinders and my engine is productive and efficient.

The revenue benefit:

Revenue is enhanced through high levels of organizational effectiveness, reduced health-care costs, reduced sick time, and the highest return on investment on the talent. When leaders put spirit in the driver's seat and ego in the passenger seat, their organization will defy the statistics showing 75 percent to 80 percent of the American workforce is doing just enough to get by. They will not suffer the revenue costs attached to stress, depression and anxiety disorders which, according to the latest research, are the fastest-growing category of disability and the top health- and productivity-related concerns for organizations.

2. The ability to be connected meaningfully to others

The business benefit (expressed as the leader and/or team member):

- ♦ I am a true team player.
- ♦ I create positive interpersonal experiences.
- ♦ I have a genuine desire to work collaboratively with others and have spirited conversations with them.
- ♦ My interpersonal behaviors create inclusion and trust.
- ♦ My communications are clear.
- ♦ I resolve conflicts openly and honestly.
- ♦ I respect the value of diversity.

The revenue benefit:
Revenue is enhanced through leveraging the diverse talents of the employees and teams. With spirit in the driver's seat, your productivity and profitability will not suffer from conditions such as these:

- ♦ 26% of American workers feel emotionally drained by their jobs.
- ♦ 28% don't have energy to do things with family or others.
- ♦ 36% just feel used up at the end of the day.

3. The ability to see life from all angles

The business benefit (expressed as the leader and/or team member):

- ♦ I see all kinds of possibilities and opportunities I did not see before.

- ♦ I have a broader perspective from which to make in-spirit-ed decisions.
- ♦ I listen, I hear, I ask, I am curious, I explore different perspectives, I seek the views of others.
- ♦ I am excited by the ideas of others.
- ♦ I synthesize my view with different views.

The revenue benefit:
Revenue is enhanced through improved strategic and tactical decisions, identification and recognition of opportunities not seen before as well as ideas and innovations that make the business more effective, efficient and profitable. With spirited leadership, your organization will defy the statistic that shows 50 percent of all business decisions fail.

Please join me in putting spirit in the driver's seat.

Every spirit counts!

About Dr. Sandy Gluckman

For more than 30 years, Dr. Sandy Gluckman has assisted leaders in aligning their organizations to deliver exceptional performance.

Recognized for her ground-breaking techniques in organizational and leadership development and corporate communications, Dr. Gluckman's approach has been described as "life changing" and "a breath of fresh air." Her techniques also have been successfully used by start-ups to multinational corporations in the U.S., England, France, Germany, Australia and South Africa.

Sandy has lectured for the Texas Woman's University Executive MBA program and the University of Dallas Graduate School of Management. She has also been published extensively in business journals, as well as being a popular guest featured in the national media. She is the author of a chapter in *Mission Possible*, published in 2003.

ACCELERATE POWERFUL LEADERSHIP PACKAGE $199.95

Monday Morning Mentoring is an expanded and enhanced hard cover version of best-selling *Monday Morning Leadership*. It includes new sessions on how to deal with change and constructive feedback. **$19.95**

Monday Morning Leadership is David Cottrell's best-selling book. It offers unique encouragement and direction that will help you become a better manager, employee, and person. **$14.95**

*7 **Moments … That Define Excellent Leaders*** The difference between average and excellent can be found in moments … literally. These moments shape the leaders we are and the leaders we will become. Seize the moment to read and apply, and you will be one step closer to leadership excellence! **$14.95**

Sticking to It: The Art of Adherence offers practical steps to help you consistently execute your plans. Read it and WIN! **$9.95**

Escape from Management Land teaches important lessons about leadership that will help you decide if you're willing to do what it takes to escape Management Land and move into Leader Land. **$14.95**

The Leadership Secrets of Santa Claus helps your team accomplish "big things" by giving employees clear goals, solid accountabilities, feedback, coaching, and recognition in your "workshop". **$14.95**

Management Insights explores the myths and realities of management. It provides insight into how you can become a successful manager. **$14.95**

Listen Up, Leader! Ever wonder what employees think about their leaders? This book tells you the seven characteristics of leadership that people will follow. **$9.95**

Monday Morning Leadership for Women is an inspirational story about a manager and her mentor. It provides insights and wisdom for dealing with leadership issues that are unique to women. **$14.95**

Leadership ER is a powerful story that shares valuable insights on how to achieve and maintain personal health, business health and the critical balance between the two. **$14.95**

Leadership … Biblically Speaking connects practical applications with scriptural guidance on how to address today's business and personal issues. **$19.95**

Leadership Courage identifies 11 acts of courage required for effective leadership and provides practical steps on how to become a courageous leader. **$14.95**

Birdies, Pars & Bogeys: Leadership Lessons from the Links is an excellent gift for the golfing executive. Zig Ziglar praises it as "concise, precise, insightful, inspirational, informative." **$14.95**

The Best Leadership Advice I Ever Got is a compilation of 75 CEOs, presidents, professors, politicians, and religious leaders describing the best advice they received that helped them become effective leaders! **$14.95**

The NEW CornerStone Perpetual Calendar, a compelling collection of quotes about leadership and life, is perfect for office desks, school and home countertops. **$14.95**

The CornerStone Leadership Collection of Cards is designed to make it easy for you to show appreciation for your team, clients and friends. The awesome photography and your personal message written inside will create a lasting impact. Pack of 12 (12 styles/1 each) **$24.95**
Posters also available.

Visit www.**CornerStoneLeadership**.com for additional books and resources.

☑ **YES! Please send me extra copies of *Who's in the Driver's Seat?***
1-30 copies $14.95 31-99 copies $13.95 100+ copies $12.95

Who's in the Driver's Seat? ____ copies X ______ = $ ______

Who's in the Driver's Seat? PowerPoint™ ____ copies X $99.95 = $ ______

Accelerate Powerful Leadership Resources

Accelerate Powerful Leadership Package ____ pack(s) X $199.95 = $ ______
(Includes one each of all items listed on page 93-94.)

Other Books

______________________ ____ copies X ______ = $ ______

______________________ ____ copies X ______ = $ ______

______________________ ____ copies X ______ = $ ______

______________________ ____ copies X ______ = $ ______

Shipping & Handling $ ______

Subtotal $ ______

Sales Tax (8.25%-TX Only) $ ______

Total (U.S. Dollars Only) $ ______

Shipping and Handling Charges

Total $ Amount	Up to $49	$50-$99	$100-$249	$250-$1199	$1200-$2999	$3000+
Charge	$6	$9	$16	$30	$80	$125

Name ______________________ Job Title ______________

Organization ______________________ Phone ______________

Shipping Address ______________________ Fax ______________

Billing Address ______________________ E-mail ______________
(required when ordering PowerPoint® Presentation)

City ______________________ State ________ ZIP ________

❑ Please invoice (Orders over $200) Purchase Order Number (if applicable) ____________

Charge Your Order: ❑ MasterCard ❑ Visa ❑ American Express

Credit Card Number ______________________ Exp. Date ______________

Signature ______________________

❑ Check Enclosed (Payable to: CornerStone Leadership)

Fax
972.274.2884

Mail
P.O. Box 764087
Dallas, TX 75376

Phone
888.789.5323

www.**CornerStoneLeadership**.com

Thank you for reading *Who's in the Driver's Seat?*
We hope it has assisted you in your quest for
personal and professional growth.

To help you facilitate teaching these concepts to your team,
a PowerPoint® slide presentation and facilitator guide is
available at www.CornerStoneLeadership.com

Best wishes for your continued success.

***Start a crusade in your organization –
have the courage to learn, the vision to lead,
and the passion to share.***